D1611795

WILDLIFE REHABILITATORS
to the RESCUE

by Meish Goldish

Consultant: Tami Vogel
Communications Director
Wildlife Rehabilitation Center of Minnesota

BEARPORT
PUBLISHING

New York, New York

West Chester Public Library
415 N Church Street
West Chester, PA 19380

Credits

Cover and Title Page, © Charlie Neibergall and © Ian West; TOC, © Micha Klootwijk/Shutterstock; 4, 5L, © John Carl D'Annibale / Times Union; 5R, © R & R Rodvold/Alamy; 6-7, © John Carl D'Annibale / Times Union; 8, © Michael Boddy/Newscom; 9, © John Gomes/Associated Press; 10, © Tiffany Young; 11, © PAUL STEPHEN/Associated Press; 12, © J. Miles Cary/Associated Press; 13, © Layne Kennedy/Corbis; 14L, 14R, © Roslyn Even; 15, © Stephanie Schmidt/Wildlife Medical Clinic; 16, 17, © Tami Vogel/WRCMN; 18T, © ALAN MURRAY/Associated Press; 18B, © Melanie Miller/Associated Press; 19, © Joel Page/Associated Press; 20T, © Jon T. Fritz/MCT/Newscom; 20B, © Charlie Riedel/Associated Press; 21, © REUTERS/Sean Gardner; 22, © MARK WILSON/Associated Press; 23, © Chuck Place / Alamy; 24, © Ana Venegas/ZUMA Press/Corbis; 25, © ZUMA Wire Service / Alamy; 26, © ZUMA Press, Inc. / Alamy; 27, © STAN HONDA/Getty; 28TL, © Gareth Fuller/AP; 28TR, © Jerry Larson/AP; 28BL, © Kelly Shimoda/Redux; 28BC, © iso Gentsch/dpa/Corbis; 28BR, © Terry Stevens; 29T, © Luke Marsden/Newspix / Rex Features; 29BL, © Imaginechina/Corbis; 29BR, © Bob Child/Associated Press; 31, © Studio MARMILADE / Shutterstock.com; 32, © Rose-Marie Henriksson/Shutterstock.

Publisher: Kenn Goin
Editorial Director: Adam Siegel
Creative Director: Spencer Brinker
Design: Debrah Kaiser
Photo Researcher: Picture Perfect Professionals, LLC

Library of Congress Cataloging-in-Publication Data

Goldish, Meish.
  Wildlife rehabilitators to the rescue / by Meish Goldish.
     pages cm. — (The work of heroes: first responders in action)
  Audience: 7-12.
  Includes bibliographical references and index.
  ISBN 978-1-61772-748-1 (library binding) — ISBN 1-61772-748-2 (library binding)
  1. Wildlife rescue—Juvenile literature. I. Title.
  QL83.2.G65 2013
  639.9—dc23
                              2012034288

Copyright © 2013 Bearport Publishing Company, Inc. All rights reserved. No part of this publication may be reproduced in whole or in part, stored in any retrieval system, or transmitted in any form or by any means, electronic, mechanical, photocopying, recording, or otherwise, without written permission from the publisher.

For more information, write to Bearport Publishing Company, Inc., 45 West 21st Street, Suite 3B, New York, New York 10010. Printed in the United States of America.

10 9 8 7 6 5 4 3 2 1

CONTENTS CONTENTS CONTENTS CO

Wounded!

In July 2009, a red-tailed hawk was resting on the roof of a building in Saratoga Springs, New York. Suddenly, a rock that had been fired from a **slingshot** flew through the air. It slammed into the hawk, knocking the bird to the ground and breaking its right wing.

This hawk had its wing broken by a flying rock.

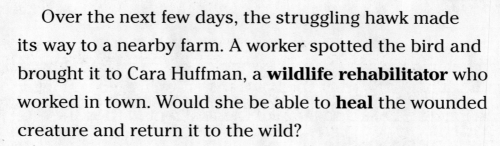

Over the next few days, the struggling hawk made its way to a nearby farm. A worker spotted the bird and brought it to Cara Huffman, a **wildlife rehabilitator** who worked in town. Would she be able to **heal** the wounded creature and return it to the wild?

Cara Huffman holds the hawk that was injured. Wildlife rehabilitators, such as Cara, are specially trained to safely handle birds like this hawk.

The red-tailed hawk is one of the most commonly seen hawks in the United States. Its **wingspan** can stretch to more than four feet (1.2 m).

In Cara's Care

Cara began to treat the hawk by wrapping its damaged wing in a soft **cast**. She hoped the cast would hold the bird's broken bones in place so that they could heal. She then housed the bird in a large crate for more than six weeks. Keeping the hawk in the crate stopped the wounded bird from flying away and breaking its wing again before it had completely healed.

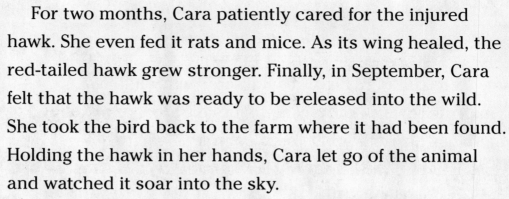

For two months, Cara patiently cared for the injured hawk. She even fed it rats and mice. As its wing healed, the red-tailed hawk grew stronger. Finally, in September, Cara felt that the hawk was ready to be released into the wild. She took the bird back to the farm where it had been found. Holding the hawk in her hands, Cara let go of the animal and watched it soar into the sky.

Cara releasing the hawk into the wild

The red-tailed haw is a **bird of prey**. It hunts and eats other animals such as mice a squirrels. It also swoops dow from the sky to catch and kil other birds in mid-flight.

On the Job

Rehabilitators like Cara Huffman help wildlife in important ways. They care for sick, injured, or **orphaned** animals until the creatures can be returned to their **natural habitat**. The animals that rehabilitators rescue are never turned into pets. Instead, they are kept only until the animals can once again live on their own in the wild.

A wildlife rehabilitator gives special care to animals in need. This owl is getting medicine because its beak was infected.

Unfortunately, some animals are too sick or injured to be returned to their habitat. They aren't able to survive on their own. As a result, they are often put to sleep so that their suffering ends in a **humane** way.

Sometimes, sick or injured animals are sent to educational centers, such as zoos. These animals are used in programs that teach visitors about wildlife.

Entering the Field

Most wildlife rehabilitators are **volunteer workers**. As a result, they are not paid a **salary**. Instead, some rehabilitators receive **donations** from people or from animal organizations. Others support themselves with their own savings or earn a living doing other jobs while working as rehabilitators part-time.

To become wildlife rehabilitators, students take classes where they learn about wild animals and how to treat them. Rehabilitator Elizabeth Hanrahan (right) is teaching a class on how to treat birds that were victims of oil spills.

Even though many rehabilitators are volunteers, they must have a **license** in order to work. Why? Most wild creatures are protected by **federal** and state laws. People who work with wild animals must know these laws. Once they do, they can get special **permits** from wildlife **agencies**.

To receive a permit, rehabilitators go through special training. They attend classes and study with an expert in the field. They also must pass written exams.

This high school senior volunteers at a rehabilitation center for birds because she wants to pursue a career working with wildlife.

A Busy House

When Birgit Sommer became a rehabilitator in Texas, she didn't know that she needed a permit to work with the squirrels in her care. After being **fined** by a **game warden**, however, Birgit got her rehabilitator license and founded Rainbow Wildlife Rescue, an operation that she ran out of her home. Her fenced-in backyard was filled with cages that housed hundreds of animals that needed her help.

One year, Birgit rehabilitated 300 animals in her care. With so many creatures to look after, it wasn't always easy for Birgit to find time to sleep. During one very busy time, she nursed birds that had to be fed every 30 minutes all day long. At night, Birgit woke up every two hours to feed baby opossums using a special tube.

A wildlife reha[bilitator] uses a feeding [tube] to give this ba[by bird] the food it ne[eds to] become healt[hy].

To feed an ani[mal] using a tube, [a] rehabilitator g[ently] pushes a soft tube dow[n] an animal's throat unti[l it] reaches its stomach. Th[e] rehabilitator can then g[ive] the animal liquid food [that] it needs to grow or hea[l].

Life in the Center

Not all wildlife rehabilitators work out of their homes. Some work in wildlife centers, which can be even busier than private houses. The Texas Wildlife Rehabilitation **Coalition** (TWRC) Wildlife Center in Houston, Texas, is a good example. This center serves as an emergency room for wildlife. Every year, people bring more than 5,000 sick, injured, or orphaned wild animals there.

About fifteen animals are brought to TWRC each day.

This baby skunk is being cared for at TWRC.

Most animals stay at the Texas Wildlife Rehabilitation Coalition Wildlife Center for only a few hours. Once an animal is treated and is no longer in danger of dying, it goes home with a rehabilitator. He or she will care for the animal until it can be released back into the wild.

At the center, rehabilitators examine the animals in order to decide how to help each one. For example, they feed animals that are too young, weak, or scared to eat on their own. They also use special equipment, such as **incubators**, to keep young or sick animals warm.

This young deer is recovering in an incubator after being hit by a car.

A Team Effort

At a wildlife center, rehabilitators do not decide on their own how to treat an animal. They work with other animal experts, including **veterinarians** and **vet technicians**. For example, at the Wildlife Rehabilitation Center of Minnesota, a sandhill crane was brought in because it couldn't fly. How did the team work together to decide how to help it?

Dr. Leslie Reed holds the sandhill crane that was brought to the Wildlife Rehabilitation Center of Minnesota. She can safely do this because the crane was briefly put to sleep in order to take X-rays. Normally, one should wear goggles and gloves to stay safe from the crane's sharp beak.

First, Dr. Leslie Reed, a veterinarian, and Chris Lewellen, a certified vet technician, examined the crane closely. They checked its eyes and studied its blood. They felt its wings for swollen **tissue** and broken bones. Finally, an **X-ray** showed that one of the wings was **fractured** due to a gunshot wound. With that information, rehabilitators were able to give the crane the proper care it needed to recover.

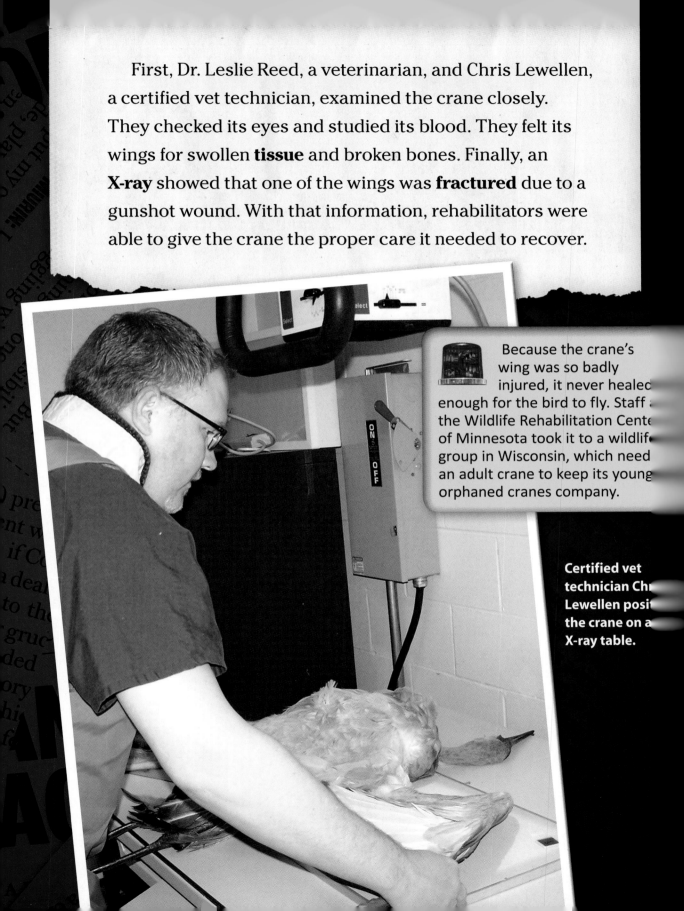

Because the crane's wing was so badly injured, it never healed enough for the bird to fly. Staff at the Wildlife Rehabilitation Center of Minnesota took it to a wildlife group in Wisconsin, which needed an adult crane to keep its young orphaned cranes company.

Certified vet technician Chris Lewellen positions the crane on an X-ray table.

Cage and Carry

When animals such as cranes must be taken from place to place, rehabilitators do not hold them in their arms. Instead, they put the animals in special containers called carriers. The carriers protect the animals and make it easier to move them around. The size and design of each container depends on the size of the animal it holds.

A worker releases a hawk from its carrier.

Twister, an orphaned black bear, leaves her carrier to return to the woods.

Animal carriers have sides with screens, bars, or holes so the animals inside can breathe and be fed.

In spring 2006, workers at a rehabilitation center in Washington State cared for several orphaned raccoons. After a few months, the raccoons had become strong enough to live on their own. In October, rehabilitators placed the animals in medium-size carriers and took them to the woods so that they could be released. Later that month, when workers were ready to release six young deer into the woods, they used tall, narrow wooden boxes so the animals could fit comfortably inside.

A seal being released from its carrier

A Deadly Spill

Rehabilitators often care for more than one creature at a time. What happens, however, when thousands of animals all need help at once? That's a **crisis** that wildlife rehabilitators faced in April 2010 when an explosion occurred on a giant **oil rig** off the Louisiana **coast**. More than 200 million gallons (757 million liters) of oil spilled into the water. In seconds, the thick, sticky oil began to **pollute** the water where pelicans, turtles, fish, and other wild animals lived.

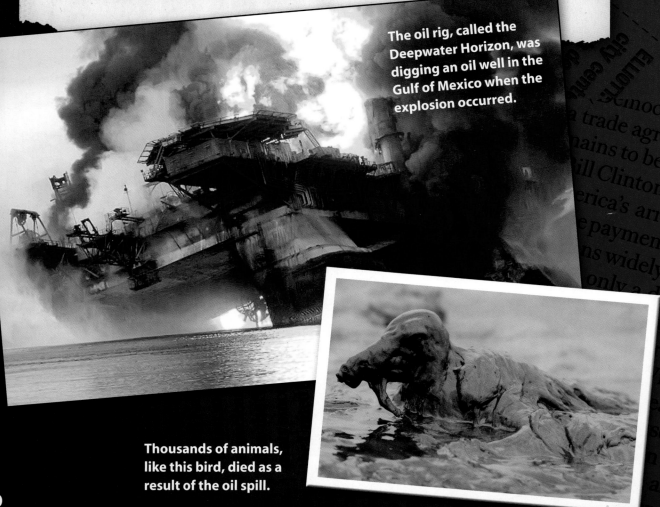

The oil rig, called the Deepwater Horizon, was digging an oil well in the Gulf of Mexico when the explosion occurred.

Thousands of animals, like this bird, died as a result of the oil spill.

Luckily, rehabilitators and veterinarians who specialize in the care of oiled wildlife were called in to help. They taught rehabilitators in Louisiana, Mississippi, Alabama, and Florida how to care for the injured animals. For example, after pelicans that had been covered in oil were captured, workers washed them in a tub using hot water and liquid soap. The clean birds were then rinsed off with a hose. Finally, the rescued pelicans were placed in outdoor pools where veterinarians watched them closely to make sure they had fully recovered. After two to three weeks, the healthy pelicans were released back into the wild.

About 1,330 oiled birds were successfully treated and released into the wild after the spill.

It took rehabilitators about 45 minutes to clean each of the rescued birds.

Teaching Others

Wildlife rehabilitators know the importance of helping wild animals in need. Yet they also know that other people, including children, need to learn why it is important to protect and rescue wildlife. That's why rehabilitators like Linda Christian of Florida often visit schools and summer camps. She and other rehabilitators teach kids how sick or injured creatures are cared for so that they can be returned to their homes in the wild.

Some rehabilitators put together programs such as this one to teach schoolchildren about owls and other wild animals.

As part of her work, Linda also shows children wild animals that have been injured so badly they cannot be released back into their natural habitat. She lets the children view the animals up close. She also takes kids to the zoo so they can learn about the animals that live there. Through her efforts, Linda hopes to teach children the importance of saving wildlife so that the animals do not become **extinct**.

Gabriele Drozdowski is a rehabilitator who teaches children about her work helping wildlife.

Some rehabilitators get special permits to keep animals that can't be returned to the wild so that they can be used to teach people about wildlife.

Wildlife Tips

One very important thing that rehabilitators like Linda Christian talk about is what to do if someone finds a sick or injured wild animal. People often wonder if they can keep the animal and care for it themselves. The answer is no. Keeping a wild animal—even a baby—without a permit is almost always **illegal**. It is also dangerous. The creature might bite people or attack pets.

An untrained person should never keep a wild animal. The creature might have a deadly disease like **rabies**, which can be passed to people and other animals through a bite.

Raccoons are animals that may have rabies. As a result, it is important that only trained rehabilitators handle them.

Many people who find a young wild animal quickly learn that they do not really know how to care for it. For example, they don't know what kind of food to give it. As a result, the animal sometimes dies.

If people find wild animals in need, they should contact a wildlife rehabilitator. The rehabilitator can provide expert care in order to return the animal to the wild. If a rehabilitator is not available, an animal **welfare** group, a zoo, or the police should be contacted to help out.

Rehabilitators know the special kinds of foods that orphaned animals need in order to become strong and healthy.

Why Be a Wildlife Rehabilitator?

A wildlife rehabilitator earns no salary, and the work is demanding. So why would anyone volunteer for the job? Ask Keirstie Carducci. She is a rehabilitator in Michigan who has helped deer, opossums, geese, coyotes, and rabbits. During the summer, Keirstie cares for up to 300 animals at a time in her barn. She says, "I'm just an animal lover, and there's such a need for it."

Wildlife rehabilitator Petra May works in Mississippi. Here, she is giving medicine to a bobcat that was struck by a car.

Bobby Horvath, a New York City firefighter, is a wildlife rehabilitator in his spare time. He knows the importance of helping animals quickly. He once saved a poisoned hawk by giving it medicine right away. "That bird was very lucky, very fortunate that it received care in a quick manner," he said. Thanks to caring individuals like Keirstie and Bobby, wildlife will continue to remain safe and protected.

Bobby Horvath shows a peregrine falcon to a group of children in order to teach them about wildlife rehabilitation.

There are about 5,000 licensed wildlife rehabilitators in the United States, and many others who volunteer to assist them.

Wildlife Rehabilitators' Equipment

Wildlife rehabilitators use many different kinds of equipment when working with animals.

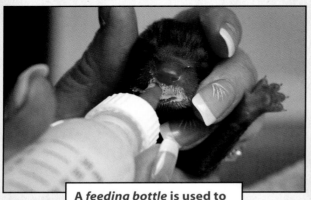

A *feeding bottle* is used to give food to some animals.

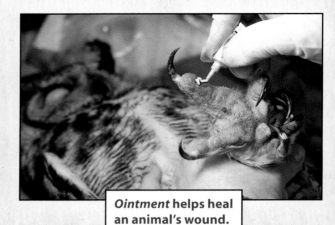

Ointment helps heal an animal's wound.

A *cast* holds an animal's broken bones in place until they heal.

Safety gloves protect a rehabilitator's hands as he or she handles and examines an animal.

A *bandage* is used to cover an animal's wound and keep it clean.

A *sleeper* serves as a soft, warm sleeping place for an animal.

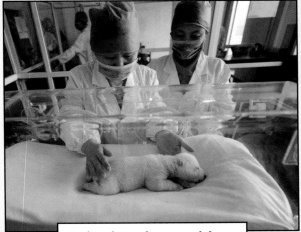

An *incubator* keeps a sick or baby animal warm and safe.

A *carrier* is used to move an animal from place to place.

Glossary

agencies (AY-juhn-seez) offices or businesses that provide a service to the public

bird of prey (BURD UHV PRAY) a bird that hunts other animals for food

cast (KAST) a cover or mold that holds broken bones in place so they can grow back together

coalition (koh-uh-LISH-uhn) two or more groups joined together for a common purpose

coast (KOHST) land that is next to the sea

crisis (KRYE-siss) a time of great danger and difficulty

donations (doh-NAY-shuhnz) money that is given to help a good cause

extinct (ek-STINGKT) when a kind of plant or animal has died out; no more of its kind is living anywhere in the world

federal (FED-ur-uhl) having to do with the national government

fined (FINED) ordered to pay an amount of money for doing something wrong

fractured (FRAK-churd) broken or cracked

game warden (GAYM WORD-uhn) a person who makes sure people obey laws relating to hunting, fishing, and the owning of wild animals

heal (HEEL) to make healthy

humane (hyoo-MAYN) kind, gentle, and caring

illegal (i-LEE-guhl) against the law

incubators (ING-kyuh-*bay*-turz) heated devices in which very young or sick baby animals are kept warm and safe

license (LYE-suhnss) a document that gives someone permission to do something or own something

natural habitat (NACH-ur-uhl HAB-uh-*tat*) the place in nature where an animal or plant lives

oil rig (OIL RIG) a platform used to drill for oil beneath the ocean floor

orphaned (OR-fuhnd) left without parents

permits (PUR-mits) written statements that give a person or group permission to do something

pollute (puh-LOOT) to make dirty due to harmful materials such as chemicals, oil, or waste being added to the air, soil, or water

rabies (RAY-beez) an often deadly disease that can affect humans, dogs, bats, raccoons, and other warm-blooded animals

salary (SAL-uh-ree) the fixed amount of money someone is paid for his or her work

slingshot (SLING-*shot*) a Y-shaped piece of wood or metal with a rubber band attached for shooting small stones

tissue (TISH-oo) masses of cells that form parts of people and animals

vet technicians (VET tek-NISH-uhnz) people who work with special equipment, often in a laboratory, to study or help animals

veterinarians (*vet*-ur-uh-NAIR-ee-uhnz) doctors who take care of animals

volunteer workers (*vol*-uhn-TIHR WURK-urz) people who work without being paid

welfare (WEL-fair) the concern for being healthy, happy, and comfortable

wildlife rehabilitator (WILDE-life ree-huh-BIL-uh-*tay*-tur) someone who cares for ill, injured, or orphaned wild animals until they can be returned to the wild

wingspan (WING-*span*) the distance between the tips of a bird's wings when they are completely outstretched

X-ray (EKS-ray) a special photo which shows the inside of a person or an animal

Bibliography

Cuny, Lynn Marie. *Through Animals' Eyes: True Stories from a Wildlife Sanctuary.* Denton, TX: University of North Texas Press (2000).

Gilbert, Suzie. *Flyaway: How a Wild Bird Rehabber Sought Adventure and Found Her Wings.* New York: Harper (2009).

Hentz, Peggy Sue. *Rescuing Wildlife: A Guide to Helping Injured & Orphaned Animals.* Mechanicsburg, PA: Stackpole Books (2009).

Jacobs, Shannon K. *Healers of the Wild: Rehabilitating Injured & Orphaned Wildlife.* Boulder, CO: Johnson Books (2003).

Read More

Chatelaine, Nancy. *Missy & Molly, Orphaned Baby Raccoons: Learning to Be a Wildlife Rehabilitator.* Big Pine Key, FL: Palm Frond Press (2009).

Curtis, Jennifer Keats. *Animal Helpers: Wildlife Rehabilitators.* Mount Pleasant, SC: Sylvan Dell Publishing (2012).

Swinburne, Stephen R. *In Good Hands: Behind the Scenes at a Center for Orphaned and Injured Birds.* San Francisco, CA: Sierra Club Books for Children (1998).

Learn More Online

To learn more about wildlife rehabilitators, visit
www.bearportpublishing.com/TheWorkofHeroes

Index

About the Author

Meish Goldish has written more than 200 books for children.
His book *Army: Civilian to Soldier* was a Children's Choices Selection in 2012.
He lives in Brooklyn, New York.